MAKE ME L...

MAGICAL MISCHIEF

JOKES THAT SHOCK AND AMAZE

by Rick and Ann Walton
pictures by Brian Gable

Carolrhoda Books, Inc. • Minneapolis

Q: Who had big ears, weighed seven thousand pounds, and married a handsome prince?

A: Cinderelephant.

Q: What did the ringmaster say when the human cannonball was shot out of the circus tent?

A: "That's going too far!"

Q: Why do trained seals always know what's happening?

A: Because they're on the ball.

Q: What do you call the trained seal when she claps her flippers?

A: The seal of approval.

Q: How do you catch a fairy?

A: Grab its fairy tale.

Show me a cowboy on a giraffe—

And I'll show you someone who is riding high.

Q: When were clocks invented?

A: Once upon a time.

Q: What do you get when the tall man substitutes for the human cannonball?

A: A long shot.

Show me a bumblebee ringing your doorbell—

And I'll show you a humdinger.

Q: What race could neither the tortoise nor the hare enter?

A: The human race.

Show me a pig in a Porsche—

And I'll show you a road hog.

Q: Why couldn't the strong man lift Alexander Graham Bell?

A: Because he could only lift dumbbells.

Q: What do tightrope-walking bears do in the winter?

A: Go into high-bear-nation.

Q: Who does the ringmaster call when someone tries to steal the show?

A: Acro-batman.

Show me a giant—

And I'll show you someone to look up to.

Q: What do you call the dancing poodle when the elephant sits on him?

A: The underdog.

Q: Did the tortoise win the race by a long distance?

A: No, he won by a hare.

Q: How do you fix a flat pumpkin?

A: With a pumpkin patch.

Show me a girl who rides sunbeams—

And I'll show you a girl who travels light.

Q: How long was Cinderella's glass slipper?

A: One foot long.

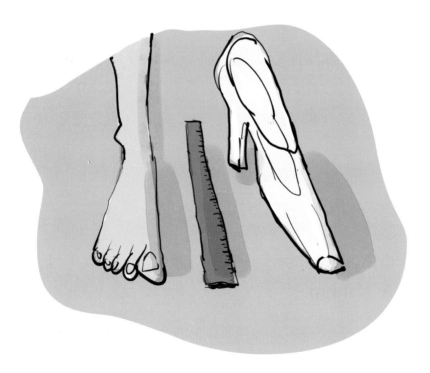

Q: Why did the ugly stepsister slap the glass slipper?

A: Because the slipper pinched her.

Show me a mamma flea—

And I'll show you a woman who's afraid that her children are going to the dogs.

Q: Why does the ringmaster like to have an artist at the circus?

A: Because an artist can draw crowds.

Q: What do you get when you cross the Frog Prince with Cinderella's footman?

A: Foot Prince.

Show me a flaming arrow—

And I'll show you a fire fly.

Q: What killed the lion tamer?

A: Cat-nip.

Q: How did the elves stay awake to make shoes all night?

A: They used sole-r energy.

Show me spiders living in your shoes—
And I'll show you webbed feet.

Clown: Don't you trust that cat?

Lion Tamer: No, she's a cheetah.

Mutt: I used to own a flea circus.

Jeff: What happened?

Mutt: All my performers went to the dogs.

Q: How do you call a leopard?

A: "Here Spot!"

Q: What fairy tale tells of a pretty girl who was ordered to clean house for a hundred years?

A: Sweeping Beauty.

Q: Why are giraffes so tall?

A: So they can sing high notes.

Q: Why do circus monkeys know everyone's secrets?

A: They hear them through the ape-vine.

Q: What do you get when you put a mousetrap in a cannon?

A: A snapshot.

Q: What fairy tale does your foot dream about when it falls asleep?

A: Sleeping Bootee.

Q: What wakes up a dragon in the morning?

A: The fire alarm.

Q: Why do clowns have flat feet?

A: Because they walk too close to the elephants.

Q: What's a pig's favorite fairy tale?

A: Slopping Beauty.

Leo: I heard the elephant trainer died from love.

Cleo: Yes, his elephant had a crush on him.

Q: Who is the loveliest lamb in all the fairy tales?

A: Sheeping Beauty.

Show me a sneezing dragon—

And I'll show you a blowtorch.

Q: Why do circuses have trained horses?

A: Because they're the mane attraction.

Q: Why did Sleeping Beauty sleep for a hundred years?

A: Because her alarm clock was broken.

Q: How do dragons weigh themselves?

A: On their scales.

Q: Why do ponies make poor ringmasters?

A: Because you can't shout if you're a little horse.

Q: Why didn't the princess sleep well on top of twenty mattresses?

A: Would you sleep well if you could fall that far when you rolled out of bed?

Q: Why did the queen decide to put a pea under the mattresses?

A: Because she was a peanut.

Show me King Kong coming out of a cannon—

And I'll show you a big shot.

Q: Why did the gorilla eat a banana skin?

A: Because it's appealing.

Q: How did Rapunzel become queen?

A: She was hair to the throne.

Show me King Kong playing cards with the Jolly Green Giant—

And I'll show you a big deal.

Q: Why did the elves make all right shoes?

A: Because they didn't want to make all wrong shoes.

Q: What happened when Puss-in-Boots went to sea?

A: He became Puss-in-Boats.

Q: And what happened when a shark got him?

A: He became Puss-in-Bits.

Q: Why doesn't the lion eat the clown?

A: Because the lion would get a funny feeling in his stomach.

Q: Why shouldn't knights wear chain mail to fight a dragon?

A: Because dragons are chain smokers.

Show me a lamb playing a tuba—

And I'll show you a bighorn sheep.

Q: What happened when the circus lions got loose?

A: A cat-astrophe.

Q: Why couldn't Tom Thumb play the piano?

A: Because he couldn't do the fingering.

Q: Why did the prince climb Rapunzel's hair?

A: Because the elevator was broken.

Show me Dracula's boat—

And I'll show you a blood vessel.

Q: Why did the lion eat the tightrope walker?

A: He wanted a well-balanced meal.

Q: What did the lion-tamer do when a giant cockroach swallowed her lion?

A: She let the cat out of the bug.

Q: Why was Rapunzel mad at the witch?

A: Because the witch kept getting in her hair.

Show me a house that has grown legs and started racing off down the street—

And I'll show you a home run.

Q: Why was the witch mad at Hansel and Gretel?

A: Because they were eating her out of house and home.

Q: Why was the human cannonball fired?

A: She was acting like a big shot.

Show me a messy pirate drinking grape juice—

And I'll show you Bluebeard.

Q: Why was Little Red Riding Hood suspicious when she saw the wolf's big nose?

A: Because she knew that something smelled.

Q: What time of year are most trapeze artists hurt?

A: In the fall.

Show me a bald giant—
And I'll show you a big wig.

Q: Why didn't the Three Billy Goats Gruff want to pay at the Troll Bridge?
A: Because it cost an arm and a leg.

Show me the skeleton of a genie—
And I'll show you a wishbone.

Q: Who did the fire-eater date?

A: An old flame.

Q: What do you get when you cross Little Red Riding Hood with a bird?

A: Robin Hood.

Q: Why did the fire-eater marry the stick lady?

A: Because they made a perfect match.

Show me a banquet for skeletons—

And I'll show you spareribs.

Q: What does a fire-eater eat with his soup?

A: Firecrackers.

Show me Dracula's safety deposit box—

And I'll show you a blood bank.

Ringmaster: I hear the fire-eater's sick. What's wrong?

Clown: She has heartburn.

Q: What do dragons do on their birthdays?

A: Light the candles and the cake and the presents . . .

Circus Manager: Have you ever been a sword-swallower before?

Job Applicant: No, but I'm willing to take a stab at it.

Q: What dragon disappeared into thin air?

A: "Poof, the Magic Dragon."

Q: Why is it so difficult to get a job as a sword-swallower?

A: Because of the cutthroat competition.

Q: How do dragons swim?

A: They do the heatstroke.

Show me a pencil that itches—

And I'll show you scratch paper.

Q: Why was the knife thrower angry?

A: The sword-swallower ate his act.

Show me King Kong's unicycle—

And I'll show you a big wheel.

Q: How do dentists fix dragons' teeth?
A: With a fire drill.

Q: What do dragons eat with their soup?
A: Firecrackers.

Q: What do sword-swallowers eat for lunch?
A: Cold cuts.

Show me a boxing banana—
And I'll show you fruit punch.

Q: Why are boring speeches like dragons?

A: Because boring speeches drag on and on and on . . .

Show me a herd of cows that plays the trombone—

And I'll show you longhorn cattle.

Q: What do you get when a dragon jumps into the ocean?

A: A heat wave.

Q: What does the glass-swallower eat when she's on a diet?

A: Lightbulbs.

Q: What happens to a knight when a dragon breathes on him?

A: He ig-knights.

Q: What does the glass-swallower eat when he craves seafood?

A: Fishbowls.

Q: Where do knights buy armor?

A: At a hard-wear store.

Q: What happened when the glass-swallower ate the window?

A: She got a pane in her stomach.

Show me a store owned by primates—

And I'll show you monkey business.

Q: Who are the two most well-respected people in the circus?

A: The tall man, whom everyone looks up to, and the sword-swallower, who's a cut above the rest.

Q: When do dragons stop eating?

A: Mid-knight.

Q: What do you call a pig who does death-defying feats?

A: A dare-deviled ham.

Q: What do you call a baby knight?

A: A knight crawler.

Q: Why are people more interested in seeing a two-headed man than a one-headed man?

A: Because two heads are better than one.

Q: What dragon ran around with Robin Hood?

A: Fire Tuck.

Q: What do you get when you cross a knight with a clown?

A: A court jouster.

Q: Who is in charge of a marionette circus?

A: The stringmaster.

Q: What kind of knight sings when the wind is blowing hard?

A: A knight-in-gale.

Q: Why is the tightrope nervous?

A: Because it's high strung.

Q: Why were the Billy Goats Gruff able to fool the troll?

A: Because hungry trolls will swallow anything.

Q: Where do acrobats learn to walk the tightrope?

A: At high school.

Q: When do most knights get hurt?

A: At knight-fall.

Q: What do you call the King of Acrobats?

A: Your Highness.

Q: How do knights see in the dark?

A: They use knight lights.

Q: What do you call a spoiled tightrope walker?

A: An acro-brat.

Q: Why don't acrobats like to get off the trapeze?

A: Because they feel let down.

Q: What did Jack's beanstalk grow?

A: Climb-a beans.

Q: What has black-and-white stripes and can swing on a trapeze?

A: A chimpan-zebra.

Q: What kind of locks won't keep people out of your house?

A: Goldilocks.

Q: What do you call trapeze artists who would rather eat than perform?

A: Snack-robats.

Q: How do snack-robats season their food?

A: With somer-salt.

Q: Where did the giant want to cook Jack?

A: In a jackpot.

Q: Why didn't the three bears eat their porridge?

A: Because they didn't have any mushroom.

Q: Which circus performers can see in the dark?

A: The acrobats.

Q: What attracts knights in shining armor even more than fair maidens?

A: Magnets.

Q: Why did the Baby Bear's chair break when Goldilocks sat on it?

A: Because it couldn't bear her weight.

Q: Why is the contortionist well liked?

A: Because she'll bend over backward for you.

Q: What did the first little pig say when the Big Bad Wolf blew down his house?

A: "That's the last straw!"

Q: Why did the tightrope walker take a duck with him?

A: So he could get down.

Q: Why did the Big Bad Wolf try to blow down the little pig's house?

A: Because he didn't have enough dynamite to blow it up.

This book is available in two editions:
Library binding by Carolrhoda Books, Inc.,
   a division of Lerner Publishing Group
Soft cover by First Avenue Editions,
   an imprint of Lerner Publishing Group
241 First Avenue North
Minneapolis, MN 55401 U.S.A.

Website address: www.carolrhodabooks.com

Library of Congress Cataloging-in-Publication Data

Walton, Rick.
   Magical mischief : jokes that shock and amaze / by Rick and Ann Walton ;
pictures by Brian Gable.
      p.   cm. — (Make me laugh)
   Summary: A collection of jokes about magic.
   ISBN: 1–57505–664–X (lib. bdg. : alk. paper)
   ISBN: 1–57505–739–5 (pbk. : alk. paper)
   Wit and humor, Juvenile. [1. Magic—Humor. 2. Jokes. 3. Riddles.] I. Walton,
Ann, 1963– . II. Gable, Brian, 1949– ill. III. Title. IV. Series.
PN6166.W35 2005
818'.5402—dc22   2003019356

Manufactured in the United States of America
1 2 3 4 5 6 – DP – 10 09 08 07 06 05